When Art Speaks to Me: A Collection of Poems

Vaidehi Patwardhan

BookLeaf Publishing

India | USA | UK

Presentation by *BookLeaf Publishing*

Web: www.bookleafpub.com

E-mail: info@bookleafpub.com

ISBN: 9789360941185

First edition 2024

DEDICATION

To the lake amidst the city chaos which witnessed this book in its making.

To the 'me' that needed to hear these words.

To my parents from whom I inherited the writer's gene.

To countless experiences and people throughout the journey who have contributed to my learning.

For every reader who resonates with the verses and finds a piece of themselves within these poems.

ACKNOWLEDGEMENT

Writing the first book and hitting the end line was anything but easy. It required constant thought stimulation, consistent reading, and immense introspection to resurface the sedimented emotions. I am grateful for the support, guidance, and encouragement from the entire team of BookLeaf Publishing. Last but not least, I thank my parents and friends who lent an ear to listen to the verses during the genesis of this book, gave constructive feedback, and pushed me toward the end line.

PREFACE

Words have the power to set us free. Although our experiences are personal to us, our stories are universal. Growing up, I realized how underrated is poetry as a healing device. It is a powerful yet simple self-expression, self-reflection, and introspection tool. Thus, it can be utilized for catharsis for everyone who finds peace within words, poetic phonetics, rhythms, and connotations. This book is for all poem lovers who perceive poetry as a way to connect their stories with everything around them and unburden themselves via its recitations.

'Our Firsts' speaks of the courage to take the first step toward what we always wanted to do but could not and encourages us to appreciate ourselves for doing all that we ever wanted to but did not. 'I hope this email finds you…' is a poetic email to be checked in the inbox of your mind. 'An Agile Aisle' is an anthem to applaud women as epitomes of independence and strength and speaks of women who wear the attire of agility throughout their lives. 'View from the Hilltop' sheds light on the dichotomies and questions one is fogged with when one finally reaches the pinnacle of anything one once wanted to but thought was unachievable. 'Counting Twenty-Five' is a cheerful ode to all those in their youth who do not wish their 20s to end ever. 'Momentary Lies' wraps up the lies we speak to ourselves yet fail to confront them as lies.

'Exploring the Hinterlands' and 'Metaphoric Colors of Loneliness' revolve around the themes of solitude and loneliness respectively and help the readers to embrace both sides of the spectrum, though not distinctly distinguishable. 'I wonder, when?' takes us back to our childhood days and provokes us to contemplate how and when our innocence and simplicity faded as we grew up. 'Then and Now' pictures blurred memories of the past lingering in the present. 'Without which, not!', 'What happened was, we grew apart' and 'Aren't we all the same?' revolve around a common theme of disconnectedness arising during unprecedented changes and underscore many similarities in human perceptions when dealing with uncertainties. 'Home away from Home' evokes an emotional tug-of-war between the mind and the heart while taking off from their motherland, soaring via the clouds of blues and landing onto an unknown land. It tries to find answers to who we are if not our home and who we are if not our family.

'A Rare Mediocrity' underscores the beauty in enduring mediocrity as simplicity, now found only in rural settings of the mind's village. 'Because the Time Speaks Irony' talks about how time, as a mystic dimension, can fool us into walking by the directions it displays at the moment, but leads us to a dead end. It highlights the paradoxical nature of time and its many shades. 'Diverse Deviance' is a poetic shout-out to everyone who dares to walk on a deviant path but fails to accept themselves as they are while walking down a road less taken. 'Thoughts as Life Rafts' metaphorically correlates the role of thoughts as rafts in life's ocean and their wave-like transient nature which propels one to reach the shore once out of sight. 'In the Winter Fall' describes a dreamlike state with lucid thoughts unraveling a few answers of a lonely mind as it takes a trip over the Louvre hall. 'To Call it a Day' evokes a rhetoric prompt to reflect upon little things that matter and are a source of real contentment at the end of the day. 'Moonlight Epiphanies' gently whispers the echoes of the soul on a serene night.

'Letters from the Past' speaks of reflections from the past in the form of letters found in the closets of an age-old almirah. 'My home is on the moon' is a poem in longing to move to the moon from the chaotic space on the earth. 'Google Search History' gives a sneak peek of what's been secretly browsed by all of us yet present in the deepest feed of our minds. 'Strums of Tanpura' tunes into the hymns of tanpura adorning its sounds on the mind's musical landscape awaiting to be synced. 'I feel restless' evokes the emotion of endless restlessness at and during times of change. 'The Sapphire Stone' shines a beam over the sapphire crystal and its beauty. 'A Garland' depicts the role of a garland in soothing our senses amidst a crowded marketplace. 'On Knowing' draws a bi-directional connection between knowing and ignorance. 'Reverse Reflections' reflects all that is and that which is not in reverse. 'I love it as much as I don't' speaks of the confusion in the duality of everything. 'An Escapade' is a poetic escape into the spaces of mindfulness. 'The Feather' paints the journey of a feather over many surfaces in its lifetime. 'The time we spend thinking' subtly explains the power of time wasted in thinking about that which is in a mere state of momentary existence.

All the poems might occur as pieces of your own stories written by you for yourself. They attempt to provide an immersive experience of emotional tapping to everyone irrespective of gender. They do not follow a specific sequence nor convey a story based on the serial order. Readers are free to pick up any poem at random which resonates with their current state of mind. Since every episode of emotional turbulence is a learning in disguise, each piece attempts to ignite the courage to become more vulnerable at least to the self if not to others, and thus tune in to the rhythms of liberation and acceptance. I hope you all imbibe the essence of this poetic state, pass it on to those you love, and reflect on your thoughts while you recite them, to birth a new poetry of your own.

Happy Reading!

Our Firsts

Fast forward and rewind, to recollect and
remind,
us of ourselves as chapters one of a kind.
Oh, this is the moment, we shall celebrate with
dining and wine,
our firsts will always push us to keep going and
shine!

This is the first time choosing a pause button
without any feign!
And up from the shallowest pit to restart all over
again!

The first time performing at a café and stepping
up the mile,
and facing criticism with a broad smile!

The first time feeling broken, lost, and lowest amidst the race,
and embracing ourselves as a work in progress!

The first time sharing the solitude with someone sweeter than that,
and flying abroad on our own for a solo trip, big fat!

The first time letting go and letting it all flow, though slow against the windthrow,
and look within to find ourselves more 'us' than we know!

The first time seeking the fearful in the quest to diminish the fear,
and cry out aloud amongst the ones near and dear!

Firsts are never the last, and they shall never be, because we are heroes in our own making, uprooted and free.

I hope this email finds you…

I hope this email finds you far away from this
email.

I hope this email finds you amidst the solitary
trees,
unbothered about future worries,
making your hair dance with the evening breeze,
and lets you release that which is required, with
ease.

I hope this email finds you unflustered about the
emails unread,
and gives you the courage to take the time to reply
and grade,
let you hold a pen to write that which goes unsaid,
and is replied to, rather than being a draft unsent,
and dead.

I hope this email embraces your eyes,
lets you confront your inner lies, teaches you to
engulf the skies,
and finds you with poetry to calm down amidst the
cries.

I hope this email finds you mouth-watering over
seasonal grapes,
and makes you laugh till your jaw aches,
helps you binge-eat your favorite cakes,
and lets you fall in love as you walk by the lakes.

I hope this email makes you smile over little joys,
and finds you with sunlight over the noise,
also finds you playing with your child with their
toys,
and gives you your 'me time' when the spring is in
poise.

I hope this email doesn't spam your inner
well-being with unsolicited opinions,
doesn't take up much of your space and clutter it
with toxic notions,
settles you well within the cushions of snowy
mountains,
and lets you celebrate yourself, just for today, near
the ponds or the fountains.

I hope this email finds you far away from this
email.

An Agile Aisle

Somewhere, right now, a baby girl is born, to a woman so strong,
her first cry filling up all the space, in the labor room as if a long song,
this moment, after all, was a moment to celebrate, a day awaited for a long,
she is named after her great-grandmother, a lady known for wit and reform,
'Idalia' was her first name with 'Rose' to tag it along.

She shines through her curls and rises through her smile,
wears a lavender scarf, and walks gracefully over an agile aisle.

Her voice is her sword, and her kindness goes
over a mile,
she perceives love not as an obligation, but as an
elixir of chamomile,
a potion she guzzles, the other half she snuffles,
makes a space for the remainder, meanwhile.

Behind the door, she scribbles during pain,
walks through a lonely lane,
gasps at a meteor falling from the sky and grins
maybe a little over a glass of champagne,
glances at the universe while gazing within her
mind's metaverse, she defines her terrain,
and does not let a stranger invade her solitude
without meeting her heart's arcane,
prays and plays, her tunes in her ways, a sight
worthy of its grandeur and restraint.

Unafraid of storms of hatred and defame,
unafraid even to counterclaim,
a nightingale of her compositions with the
composure of a rising flame,
traverses through the valleys of vain and disdain,
all on her own, though an unfair game,
treats it all fair and beats with a rare layer of
flare and glare, her brows speak of an exclaim,
creates a room of her own, wears a tinge of
musk and cologne, pays off her bills, a grande
dame.

Her fingers caress the soft petals of jasmines and
roses, of flowers in every season,
subtly rising at an equal level, in the Age of
Reason,
cheers to her in all sizes, colors, races, and every
vocation,
a salute in honor of her strength, a loud
jubilation,
she is the force of creation, at many levels of
divine revelation.

View from the Hilltop

What does it look like from the hilltop?
Solitary?
An escort.
Isolated?
Like a dot.
Unencumbered?
Maybe,
or maybe not.

What does it look like from the hilltop?
Gratifying?
Long sought and kind.
A nook corner?
Beyond the hustle so blind.

Like a terrific sight?
That's right.
Promiscuous. Rewarding. Undefined.

What does it look like from the hilltop?
Do you sense a dichotomy?
To fly, fall, or jump, I can't decide.
Do you foresee?
An unforeseen agony.
Is it a tunnel or a valley?
A tunnel stretched across the plains of
monotony.
It looks like a valley too, a tumultuous dive in
mahogany.

Let us meet at the hilltops,
and let's not hesitate,
to speak a word or two.
Let's exchange some stories,
of our journeys, not in haste,
but by the bonfires,
or under the open skies,
and let our conversations brew.

Counting 'Twenty-Five'

'Twenty-Five' year blend -
Oh, please lend, without a bend or an end.
Is it the youthful flare and glare,
or the cuckooing soul confused in blare?
Lessons learned and unlearned,
over the quarter with amends and contend.
Is it or is it not,
that the radiance in eyes and confidence in
speech are so rare?

Observe and notice the signs of the universe,
do not worry if you fail,
drift adrift unplanned but not miffed,
to attain a state hearty and hale.
Stay not alone if you can't,
no substitute to the love you shall derive,

simplify that which is not, also let that which is,
an innate trait to revive.

Attend the inner demons, the monologues,
the voices and desires so large,
it's okay to fail sometimes to be your
cheerleader,
and seek help to charge.
Ace the art of conversations and engage.
Smile at strangers and get outside the cage.
Practice gratefulness towards those who stayed.
Also, towards those who didn't, for all, teach a
lesson as an aid.

Pause, stop, lie down for a while,
reflect, rewrite, introspect in prospect, and
retrospect over the mile.
Find your niche, an extraordinary in the
collective ordinary,
as long as you are, in your own eyes, always
legendary.
Learn, absorb, digest, and assimilate the idea of
detachment,
you don't get a penny for a lost and wasteful
sentiment.
Binge more on ice creams, waffles, cornettos
and blueberries,
cupcakes and munchkins will also add to a lousy
day, a blissful spoon of cherries.

Paint, read, sing, and hop on to the tunes of your
favorite drum beats,
if not all this, roll to the rhythms of silences in
disguise all over the night streets.
Reply, respond, react, and retract, decide only
when necessary,
and be brave enough to quit and leave that which
isn't so merry,
your mind and body aren't the punch bags, but a
lifelong love sanctuary.
Do peep outside the window to defenestrate, at
the darkest and lowest of all times.
Yes, you did untap into the priceless world of
contentment, happiness, and peaceful chimes.

Fear not the aloneness, for even the knee, in its
circular socket,
is not aware that there is another one, just like it,
just an inch away.
It's okay to feel clueless sometimes, and start
searching for the lost locket,
question everything, find answers, validate, and
rewrite them, sometime in the day.
Age is just a number, and even if not, you keep
looking forward and get set,
for the years ahead hold treasures of joy, so
cherish everything, and replay!

Momentary Lies

Forward Momentum?
Necessary to negate,
the ill luck described in an illegible vignette.

Sideways Momentum?
Auxiliary to liberate,
and open the gate.

The net worth of our bodies?
For the digital watches to estimate
and the treadmill runs and ellipticals to rate.

Step up the ladders?
With no room to move around, but wait.
A summit, as transient as a buffer state!

Neat shoes and tidy ties?
And something else to obligate.
Formals to impress, forced smiles - innumerate.

Are these the rules in a set?
To accelerate.
Then, let's check and calculate.
The spreadsheet failed to compute and get,
a total of happiness as a net.

So relish the moments with a wine and a pet,
dress up and shine in a cozy silhouette,
restart and reset, and don't forget,
to collect the momentary lies of needs unmet,
here and there, spilled over a wide carpet!

Metaphoric Colors of Loneliness

Loneliness is like an inescapable void,
a dusk time making us paranoid!

Loneliness is a hollow cave,
like a rigid fence built by someone brave!

Loneliness sounds like silences between breaths,
like an ocean with unfathomable depths!

Loneliness is an hourglass full of sand,
appearing like an enchanted island!

Loneliness is an emotion as demanding as
connectedness,
a soft corner haunting the room full of mess!

Loneliness is like an incoherent poetry,
waiting to be heard but lost in its mystery!

Loneliness is a cozy blanket on a winter night,
craving for cuddles and kisses uptight!

Loneliness has but many antidotes for us to
survive,
like a cacophony of nature blessing us to thrive!

Loneliness is not easy to navigate through,
when endless thoughts haunt us in a queue!

It is but loneliness which spirits us with wisdom,
with hope, power, and a brand-new custom!

I Wonder, When?

An apple, a balloon seller, a hand peacock,
a magic pot, a jingle, board games - an entire
stock!
I wonder when we stopped revisiting this nook,
with endless stories of our childhood now found
only in a slam-book!

Cotton candy, melody, mango bite, ice cream
filling,
annual gathering, and flag hoisting, those days
were truly freewheeling!
I wonder why we stopped revisiting this nook,
the rear mirror reflecting our naive look!

Listening to stories of her times from granny
alongside played tunes of looney,
bread butter jam - a luxury, sleep routine with
Bugs Bunny!
I wonder how we stopped revisiting this nook,
gumboots, raincoats, and a Bumbershoot hung
onto a distant hook.

Hide and seek, strawberry-strawberry, polo and
rummy,
with vacations so long, and ice candies so
yummy!
I don't wonder anymore about the nook.
Because even knocking on our neighbor's door
now makes us shook.

Then and Now

Then, these plants,
listened to us in the backyard,
and birthed our conversations,
endless and unmarred!
Now, somehow these creepers,
are charred by lack of light.
They can't fight nor resist fright,
against their shadows at night.

Then, these roses,
bloomed in the pursuit of hope,
now, somehow its colors have faded,
under intense heat, they can't cope.
Then, with their nearness we were humbled,
with their thorny appearances.

Now, in need of their company,
we foresee remoteness.

Then, in the same backyard,
we threaded the fabric of our days,
we designed then, an apparel jaded and
unscarred,
now, somehow, we unweave but the same cloth
in case,
the doors to this yard aren't unbarred!
Then, these sunflowers,
gazed at the sun in the hope of erasing the
gloom,
now, somehow their progenies can't withstand,
uncertain hours of doom in the womb.
Then, during the unsought weather,
the grasshoppers danced with joy to the sounds
of thunders,
now, somehow they are chapfallen,
while hopping on their feathers.

Then, these jasmines
were affected by the solitary haze,
now, somehow this solitariness
has turned into a state they fully embrace.
Because the then and now shall always emerge,
together, but in a separate phase!

Home Away from Home

Back to the roots, to being self-grounded,
with a home away from home of lucidity and
pampering,
to seek the strength oddly old yet new-founded,
a craving, an ache, a knowing, all compounded.

A journey from take-off to landing,
to home away from home safe-guarded with
love,
an act of balance, an act of finding,
an ode to the dreamland, a faithful yearning.

A flower almost bloomed, a flower in longing,
to become a bud again,

at home away from home of comfort and
belonging,
a rescue from loneliness, a rumble, and gonging.

A place, a place in time, the people of that time,
a three-dimensional space with a steep climb,
to the home away from home of soft cushions
and straight spine,
a familiar abode with endless memories
entwined.

The flight is taken, a leap in disguise,
amidst the tiny mansions, the square-fields that
despise,
the home away from home of microscopic size,
now so distant with all its lies.

Through the white clouds to the land unknown,
through the spaces between the knuckles torn
and outgrown,
through the glimmer in the eyes so lone
unshown,
to outshine the older version, yet another
milestone,
a vault over to another home far away from the
home.

A Rare Mediocrity

Far beyond the distinct hills, there is a village,
where folks communicate only with letters.
They worship the existence of breath in vintage,
sit by a pond and observe as they age,
how ducklings radiate symmetric ripples,
upon taking their first leap in their rivage.
After all, to swim adrift,
with slowness and ease as their innate privilege!

They inhale solace under the shades of mulberry
trees,
and exhale the yesterdays by the shores and the
sea breeze,
their skin has layers to absorb but also to resist,
that which doesn't appease,

for absorbance makes them wise,
and resistance leads to a lack of disease!

They welcome an acquaintance,
without any tease,
lend them ears, and a cup of 'kahawa',
on a carpet of leaves,
bid them along with a smile to carry to the city,
and a bunch of wooden keys,
to open the door of the mind's village, a rare
mediocrity.

Because Time Speaks Irony

Time glorifies its lies,
and spills off an ambiguity,
yet we trust that which demands to be trusted,
but aches in the extremity.
In that instance,
melancholy births creativity;
breathes anew a meaning,
discorded from a meaningless beauty.

It is when the sun rises,
and sets and rises again,
the magic of repetition and routine,
is realized by those who are sane.
And when the moon exhibits cyclicity,
in seasons of vain and disdain,
the power of renewal and redemption,
is realized with grace in the thick of pain.

Because time speaks irony,
it disguises its tenderness as bitterness,
it creates pearls and defines the oysters,
within the shell with finesse.
It uproots that which neither was justified,
nor attempted to serve the race,
and is bleak, armored,
and unchanged, so dare not to chase.
Spiraling along back and forth,
then to and fro, and the highs and lows,
within the school rooms and pool rooms,
clubrooms and music rooms in compose,
a nostalgic fog clouds the brain,
and isn't a forte to cherish or keep close,
then surely is the present a gift,
to unwrap and drift into the momentary prose.

We lost a million, we gained but a penny,
we admired the followers but lost the ferry,
which travels miles and isn't afraid of storms,
which sails along the path and floats airy,
deceptions deceive deep down along the track of
time,
our hopes into the mystic-chimeric rosemary,
for loving and giving with denials and
rejections,
make a perfect formulary, in time and its glory.

Diverse Deviance

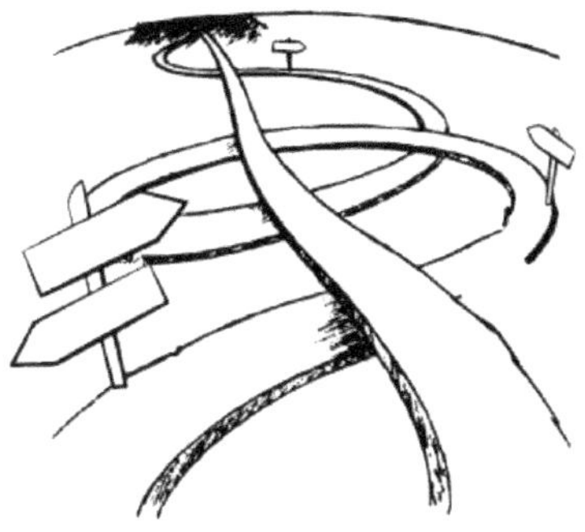

This is for the deviant in you,
who marches onto a diverse path,
partakes in the savories tasted by a few,
unruffled by the flavors of the aftermath.

This is for the deviant in you,
who fights with a forthright thought,
takes a flight with an untold crew,
unbothered by the routes, unknown and
unsought.

This is for the deviant in you,
who does not retrace imprints of the footprints,
of those who walked this path anew,
and spilled over a few misguiding hints.

This is for the deviant in you,
on the way to a point unknown,
touched by very few,
filled with insights and wisdom of one's own.

This is for the deviant in you,
by the deviant in me and all of us,
an applaud in silence, a hug from a distance,
a branch of a shaky tree to rest on, for instance,
an answer to ourselves, a roar in vengeance!

What happened was, we grew apart

What happened was, we grew apart,
so we lost faith in living,
the daily notions of waking up strong-headed,
and sleeping back to the coffee brewing.

Long mirror stares and the bizarre murmurs,
distinguished yet blurred,
a constant struggle to smile,
while we're suffering through an emotional
afterward.

Isn't it time, to let the curtains unveil the sacred
truth,
before the dusk takes over!

What happened was, we grew apart,
so we stopped embracing the space,
and stopped scarring the blankness of the page
with our clumsy pen,
and never let it trim its wings with an ace.

It's of no consequence, however,
if we stayed there in the middle of nowhere,
for we are complete through the openings we
made,
but couldn't close them, fair!

Thoughts as Life Rafts

A capillary was found within the limbic regions,
tensile enough to entwine intuitions,
with elapsed affairs, stories of nightmares,
and upbringings in many layers,
synthesizing a life raft so rare,
as unmoored as thoughts of scare.

Stacked and piled,
they arose on the surface uninvited,
on most of the days, unreasonable and defiled.
They kept the go-getters afloat, clear-sighted,
undrowned, ongoing, and wild,
some of them carried even,
to a shore unreached and lighted.

These, since the dawn of humanity,
were always intangible and unbeaten.
Maybe, a chunk of these in integrity,
comforted us in return,
maybe, during times of perplexity,
love was their buoyancy,
and subtle reflections of us through them,
a reliable guide much long forgotten!

Without which, not!

The sky is still the same.
And, the birds whisper the same name.
The sky is still the same and the birds whisper
the same name,
it's us who dwindled to fit in,
within a collaged and collective frame!

We've dropped behind the shawl,
while we glanced everywhere all along.
We've dropped behind the shawl, while we
glanced everywhere all along,
it's us who parted our ways disguised,
as an exemplar, to obey and to belong!

We've hid behind the tall bush,
the place we sought as a muse.
We've hid behind the tall bush, the place we
sought as a muse,

it's us who segregate our daily jitters,
from a bowl full of unordinary blues!

We entail a similar sense.
To foster in us a radical change.
We entail a similar sense, to foster in us a radical
change,
it's us who write and it is us who dictate
and do not dare to leave, even if we can, our
cage!

Aren't we all the same?

Aren't we all doomed,
within the brightness of the sun and the darkness
without it?
Oh, the audacity of the human race exhumed,
to forget the co-passengers in this lifetime, in
less than a micro-minute!

Aren't we all fools,
in the length of the day and the width of the
night?
Oh, the audacity of the human race with its
rules,
to question its existence at sight!

Aren't we all greedy for a witness,
to our pain, happiness, accomplishments, and
emergence into new?
Oh, the audacity of the human race to showcase
the failure to harness,
to absorb the pointlessness in a meaningful web
we weave!

Aren't we all the broken pieces of the puzzle?
Do we design it on our own?
Oh, the audacity of the human race to stay in its
bubble,
when it doesn't turn out exactly for what it is
sown!

Aren't we all the same, or are we not,
when life necessitates an amalgamation?
Oh, the audacity of the human race to
metamorphose and rot,
with the allowance to accept the nothingness in
elation.

Exploring the Hinterlands

Nothing is more devouring,
as the tastes of oneness one indulges into,
for even the largest of symphonies fall short
when compared,
with the essence of solitude, one's soul evokes
to!
Nothing is more calming,
when one becomes settled in one's own
company,
for all, we are by ourselves till the breath our
heart beats to!

Nothing persists beyond the depths,
of the ever-witnessing ocean,
nothing persists above the pervasive wings,
of the skies in motion,
nothing achieves a shape, neither color,
and nor even a perception of attrition,
for all, we float on, are moments in an expanse
with a well-directed mission!

Nothing within the seeming,
nor anything beyond the needful knowing,
there is not much beige to unveil the emergence,
of the shades in mourning,
nothing too complex, nor so simple,
and nor a comprehensible pact for signing,
for all, we are bound and unbound, in the
mysterious law of becoming and growing!

Are we all worthy enough or are we not,
to witness the stillness,
and the momentary stroke of time,
so lasting when felt and perceived, so windy yet
windless!
Not so alone is the bread loaf, nor is the lying
pillow,
none of them even, have any grievances,
for all we are just touched by the now in the
now, not softly, nor bluntly,
but in zones beyond our mere senses!

In the winter-fall

The air whispered in rapid-fire French,
like an indecipherable entrance to the Paris
Louvre.
As frozen music, it was so all-consuming -
the departing tail lights, the mist of the
fountains,
a transparent pyramid, with an enormous trench.

Stocky and dark, through the revolving door,
was only the beginning of the Louvre itself,
like the aisle of a dark movie theater.
The yawning space with the honey-colored
stone,
a crypt-like atmosphere, all leading to a mellow
tour.

As I gazed down the murky corridor,
over the paintings in relative darkness,

I sensed something similar in all of them,
an oppressive quality of slowly adjusting to the
dark,
an arid essence of lurking hope, and the bustling
sounds of roar.

To focus on anything within only the four walls,
was similar to an elevator jolted to a stop,
built with few stones of doubts and mourns.
Perhaps, everywhere at all but here,
were elevations towards the highest calls.

The contention was weirdly logical after all,
to stay ablaze, within the night of stark
awakening -
'We are all in this together now, we are all one'.
Moments later, the light diminished through the
door,
as I dreamt of a dream, of Louvre Hall, back in
the winter fall.

To Call it a Day

What's all that one can ask for to call it a day?
Is it the solace in the sunsets,
and silences by the bay?
Or is it the rush, the hurries, mighty worries,
and daydreams, you say?

What's all that one can ask for to call it a day?
Is it stopping by the lakes,
embracing the dollops of dewdrops in the way?
Or is it the drags, the stretches, the lifts, the
pulls,
unfulfilled with nods to opinions, you can't
weigh?

What's all that one can ask for to call it a day?
Little gains, lingering drizzles of half-seen
visions,

though pointless at the moment and within the
zone of gray?
Or the beginning of its bloom only if watered,
looked after, and molded, as if clay?

What's all that one can ask for to call it a day?
Ticking off the checklists, reaching the numbers,
and fulfilling the deadlines and commitments
right away?
Or the coffee breaks, going by the desks,
lending an ear, a bite of chocolate, or a
sunflower smiling at a ray?

What's all that one can ask for to call it a day?
Take for granted that we are destined with,
gifted, and blessed,
or being grateful instead, drop an effortful sweat,
relay?
With no fret to let, and get set, win the bet,
dissolve the wants, diminish the wars, and
forgive the wrongs of yesterday?

Moonlight Epiphanies

When the horizon chants a sacred psalm,
it sprinkles the joys of the catalytic calm,
and unfurls in harmony a dusky endeavor,
one can fancy to entice and imbibe, forever.

Come, take a look at the eventide realm,
which whispers a gospel to savor,
in favor of the peace in its transient charm,
one can flaunt about and let go, never!

Shedding the old layers,
emerges anew a shredded tree,
For the sky stands an all-encompassing witness,
to applause for this magical event, you see.

Come, feel the poetic urge invading the soul,
like a thread purges the needle,

while surfaces up an immense joy,
from a jar of solitude like a lotus in a puddle!

With an ardent breath, one breathes,
and an enchanting energy one emits, so lit,
how meditative is this impulse,
which subtly flows along the chaotic thought pit!

Come, take a glimpse at the blooming flowers
within,
as if an embracing spring,
as long as one longs for the divine,
to come here and bring -
The stronger, happier, and healthier versions
beneath,
one can only fall and keep falling in love, in a
heartbeat!

Waypost the midnight hour ticks the clock,
with no signs of sleep, and don't yet sleep,
for one is all pumped up to check in,
with the promises, they are determined to keep!

Come, sense the pulse of these silences,
one is destined to be one with,
Oh, how sad, for even the words here don't
justify,
the beauty of the moment's zenith!

Letters from the Past

The age-old almirah standing aghast,
sturdy enough to last,
as an abode to a few letters from the past,
written by my old self to me now, steadfast!

Somehow, they whisper names just lying on the
floor,
in some form unknown, or barely felt anymore.
The texture is bleak, with an unpolished cover,
like a pale sky with a fading candor.

The language of what's gone, of what outshines,
is so facile to be read, that it is lost in a maze.
'Accept it just as it sounds, without reading
through the lines.

Go into the depths where life takes a rise', it
says.

The stillest hours of night hold these letters,
well with an embrace.
What we loved and lost, lived and experienced,
after all,
was a submerged sensation of an ample past, an
uncommon place.

My home is on the moon

We are proud to be the residents of the moon
my poetry and the art are its only occupants
Now I know how it feels like to stay here
We have too many spaces to be filled with colors
Too many gaps and shapes alike to be merged
It's been like that for a while now, maybe a few
hours
I recognize how it feels to be left like this
It wasn't an easy portrait to sketch
I hide away everything else, but the colors and
palettes
few strokes of oil pastels, maybe, to cover the
wounds

I feel no gravity of pain, my tears don't stay on
my face
the colors float, formlessly, unbothered to fill the
canvas
I look at the earth and I think of never going
back there
Because it was not somewhere I could
effortlessly cope
It was just a ball of worries and despair, with no
remainder of hope
That which I need not carry on the moon,
Because the moon is my new home!

Google Search History

Book cafes for breakfast with a friend. Cat café studios. Art workshops and some more.
Metaphors for grief, oxymorons to ace at sarcasm, epiphanies by a seashore.
Signs he is into me and signs he is ghosting me.
Sites to enroll for a part-time job if I have to afford the fee.
Coping mechanisms to get outside of this state and feel that I belong.
Art of Living courses and fees, a bit of therapy to tag along.
How should I cut someone off? How do I know that I am cut off?

How to bluff and talk at a party, how to fake a
laugh?
Is the Kaliyuga near its ending? Are these
answers found in the 'The Krishna Key'?
The Economic Times, The Reader's Digest, The
Times of India, and The Speaking Tree.
Does God exist? Would spirituality or science
ever bring peace?
What do real death experiences feel like? Is
dying a process that happens with ease?
25 things to do before I turn 25.
Can a time machine halt this age? If not, what
else can I buy?
Why do my fingers tremble? Is this a symptom
of an anxiety attack?
Poetries to calm down. Subscription to Spotify
with a premium pack.
Pills to alleviate the insomnia, quick fixes to get
over some fears.
Why do I cry so much? Is there an endless
source of my tears?
Book Summary of Virginia Woolf's 'A Room of
One's Own'.
Can't I be like her, a woman of age with wisdom
and a funny bone?

Strums of Tanpura

I hold it on my lap,
on a dusky evening,
raise my hand to tune it,
and gaze at its length,
I wonder about its history,
of the maestros who played it,
sing a few hymns as I strum its strings,
alongside a rhythm tap.

It reverberates and it awakens within,
a lingering tune of nature's artistry,
a magical cone of a mystic beam,
its sounds transcend the visible bonds,
and take up the space with an invisible thread,
as I close my eyes to murmur a few thumris,
I weave dreams with every stroke, with a wide
grin.

It is a prayer to the universe,
each time with each pluck,

with each of its strings revealing a bit,
of the echoes of the ancient corridors,
its wooden body is a strong witness,
to countless ragas and melodies,
an artist's armor, a mandatory attire,
a rare friend to a poetic verse.

I feel restless

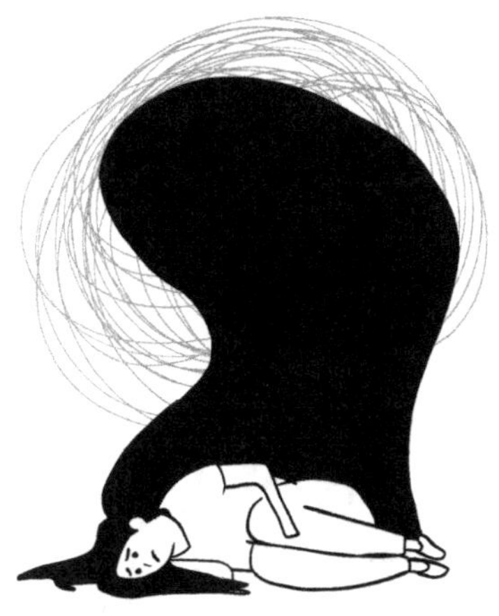

I feel restless,
to dismantle old thoughts,
to walk onto a solitary road,
takeoff from my shoulders,
the purse full of burdened love.

I feel restless,
to get rest again,
to rejoice in the eternal,
to survive the cold,
during winters marked by passion.

I feel restless,
in the wind-blown land,
bearing the weight of raindrops,

in the great quiet of distances,
when my letter is long unanswered by you.

I feel restless,
in the first moment of brightness,
when my eyes draw some refreshment,
to begin the day in search of a meaning,
to run to nature upon its call.

I feel restless,
to taste a fruit of the new season,
understand its multiplicities and complexes,
to love the questions themselves,
like locked rooms and unsung songs.

I feel restless,
to drink the solitude,
to wait for the incidental hours,
to crack open the nut,
of unrest around us!

The Sapphire Stone

A September birthstone,
an artist's muse,
a jeweler's jewel.
In its light,
even the skies feel blessed.
No moonlight cuts the air.
In its charm,
even the trees on the hills,
dance on their own.

A healer's crystal,
in many colors of sapphire,
the star within the gem,
speaks of creation,
speaks of a blend,
of the beauty of the stardust,
of us to shine,
within the oneness and laughter.

A Garland

Amidst the flower market,
a garland greeted me,
and exhaled the fragrance,
of calm and embrace,
I inhaled it to my finest capacity,
and held it in my palms,
I was eager to deck it in hair,
as much as the garland wished to stay there,
I wore it while there was time,
and as soon as I did,
it was muted and sullen,
and heavily laden,
with conventions and folklore.
The flowers turned pale and flabbergast,
lost their colors and odors of the past,

petal by petal they left their tribe,
of beauty and hype, in sassy delight.
The flowers that I wore had filled me,
however, with breath more fragrant than its scent,
and a momentary spell of a blissful ascent.

On Knowing

I no longer know,
how human interaction feels like,
I no longer remember,
how spending time with someone looks like,
I no longer feel,
how an emotion emerges,
I can no longer decide,
whether an emotion is pure even or just a spike,
I no longer crib,
over the dreams on strike,
I no longer live by,
that which conditioned my psyche,
to be, to do, to act, to think, all alike,
I no longer know,
that I know for sure,
whether knowing is truth or full of lies.
Is it a condition of bliss or ignorance in
disguise?

Reverse Reflections

It is where others see you as weak, you create
strength.
It is where others see you as a failure, you are a
success.
It is where others support you, you lack support.
It is where others oppose you, you become
harmonious.
It is where others see you happy, and you are
sad.
It is where others see you calm, you are angry.
It is where others help you, you are helpless.
It is where others see you in abundance, that you
feel lacking.

It is where others see you as lacking, you are in
abundance.
It is where others stop knowing you, you start
learning yourself.
It is not where it is not, it is where it is not.
For everything is but a reverse reflection of
itself.

I love it as much as I don't

I love all I create,
as much as that I let abate.
Just like a mother loves all her children,
without any debate.
I feel my cellulite,
as much as I embrace the softness of my skin.
I admire the dark circles under my eyes,
through all I have been.
I embrace the garden of my mind,
even if I can't water it by myself.
I nourish my eyelids even if,
they choose not to let me sleep.
I learn the language of my thoughts,
though it is incomprehensible sometimes, and
bleak.
I listen within to the noise I sense,

as much as I crave the silence.
I greet the guests well,
as much as I wish to remain in my shell.
I love it as much as I don't,
for this is the skill I've finally honed.

An Escapade

A narrow street,
lighted with kerosene lamps,
bearing painted walls with graffiti art,
spoke of people who had walked down this alley
before,
at an offbeat.

A painted vase,
with the darkest of its secrets within,
bearing space for the flowers that bloom,
spoke with reverence for the artists who painted
it,
an epitome of grace.

The 21st floor balcony,
felt a little closer to the sky,
bearing the secrets of the people who vented out
to it,
spoke of its role as a companion during
loneliness,
an alluring alchemy.

A series of monographs,
like bundled letters written by the poets to
others,
bearing more realities than their inheritance or
upbringing,
spoke of steps to be followed to unlock the
subliminal,
and long-coveted maps.

A mansion within woods,
with a front yard layered with hues of the hills,
bearing the sounds of silences,
spoke of nature and its rules,
its neighborhoods.

The Feather

The Feather,
dances with the breeze,
air is its only rhythm.

Singing at the pitch,
of the nature with its lyrical cadence,
it praises its artistry.

Steadily it wavers,
unafraid of the path,
the wind is its only guide.

Occasionally it ends,
on the ground,
to start flying again.

Silently it touches,
the skin of the pale,
and renews it with softness.

Slowly it drops,
in the basket of flowers,
smells their company.

Touching the skies,
the branches and dust alike,
it doesn't lose its sight.

Hoping to land in solitude,
at a place where its presence,
is honored with tenderness.

The time we spend thinking

The time we spend thinking we are all alone,
is the time wasted and torn.
The time we spend thinking about our existence
is the time formed in the womb of all the
seasons.
The time we spend thinking we are all just a
speck of dust,
is the time projecting a beam on every particle as
it must.
The time we spend thinking we are immortal
is when we encounter death and face the
subliminal.
The time we spend thinking that we are all
separate

is the time revealing its intersection with our
fate.
The time we spend thinking about the time we
are left with
is the time that unfolds its meaning and myth.

www.ingramcontent.com/pod-product-compliance
Lightning Source LLC
LaVergne TN
LVHW050924200726
843508LV00011B/2270